I0814900

POLITICAL SYSTEMS IN ACTION

DEMOCRACY

From Ancient Greece to the American Dream

ALEX WEBB

Published in 2025 by **Cheriton Children's Books**
1 Bank Drive West, Shrewsbury, Shropshire, SY3 9DJ, UK

First Edition

Author: Alex Webb
Designer: Paul Myerscough
Editor: Sarah Eason
Proofreader: Anna Chambers

Picture credits: Cover: Doodle Press. Inside: p4: Shutterstock/Vesperstock, p5: Shutterstock/Saikat Paul, p6: Wikimedia Commons/Hans Holbein the Younger, p7: Shutterstock/Alexandros Michailidis, p8: Shutterstock/Bill Perry, p9: Shutterstock/Krikkiat, p10: Shutterstock/David Smart, p11: Shutterstock/Everett Collection, p12: Wikimedia Commons/John Trumbull, p13: Wikimedia Commons/John Trumbull, p14: Shutterstock/Everett Collection, p15: Wikimedia Commons/Alexander Gardner, p16: Shutterstock/Murathakanart, p19l: Wikimedia Commons/Leon A. Perskie, p19r: Wikimedia Commons/Yousuf Karsh, p20: Shutterstock/Andrea Izzotti, p21: Shutterstock/Michael Tubi, p22: Shutterstock/Steven Frame, p24: Shutterstock/Maverick Pictures, p25: Wikimedia Commons/The Suffragette, p26: Shutterstock/Ryan DeBerardinis, p27: Shutterstock/Maria Agustinho, p28: Shutterstock/4kclips, p29: Shutterstock/Andrew F. Kazmierski, p30: Wikimedia Commons/Library of Congress, p31: Shutterstock/Ground Picture, p32: Wikimedia Commons/U.S. National Archives and Records Administration, p33: Shutterstock/Chictype Montreal, p34: Shutterstock/Nick Fox, p35: Shutterstock/ART Production, p36: Shutterstock/Drop of Light, p37: Wikimedia Commons/President of the Russian Federation, p38: Shutterstock/Rob Crandall, p39: Shutterstock/Lev Radin, p40: Shutterstock/360b, p41: Shutterstock/Jose Hernandez/Camera 51, p42: Shutterstock/Gil Corzo, p44: Shutterstock/Michael Puche, p45: Shutterstock/Connie Guanziroli.

Printed in the United States of America

Please visit our website,
www.cheritonchildrensbooks.com
to see more of our high-quality books.

Contents

CHAPTER 1

The Story of Democracy

A democracy is a form of government in which ordinary people take part in governing, or running, their country. The idea of democracy was first expressed in ancient Greece, and the word "democracy" comes from the Greek language: "Demos" means people, and "krates" means rule, so "democracy" means "rule by the people." In a democracy, a group of people decide how their community should be run. President Lincoln (1809–1865) defined democracy as "the government of the people, by the people, and for the people."

Two Main Types

There are two main types of democracy: a direct democracy and a representative democracy. In a direct democracy, every citizen has the right to make laws and decisions together. This can work well in a small, simple community. In a whole country, it is impossible to gather everyone together to make decisions all the time. Modern societies are also complex, so the people who make the decisions require some expert knowledge. This is why direct democracies, in which all the citizens of one country vote on all decisions made, are not suitable for governing most countries.

The United States has a representative democracy in which each person is entitled to vote for a representative who will make laws and decisions for the whole country.

These women are lining up to vote in an election in India. They have ID cards to prove their identity and their right to vote in their country.

Choosing and Voting

In a representative democracy, the people of a community choose, or elect, representatives to make the laws and decisions for them. At national level, the representatives are politicians, such as members of congress. The people choose their representatives in elections every few years, in which all citizens may vote. In office, the representatives must represent the views of the people who elected them. If the people do not approve of their decisions, the representatives can be voted out of office at the next election. This ensures that, although the people of a country or state do not vote on every decision made, the final authority belongs to the people.

DEMOCRACY: PAST AND PRESENT

In this book we will look at the political system of democracy, its history, and its place in the world today. We'll compare democracy past with democracy present, and look at some of the key figures of this political system in the People and Politics features. Look out too for the Democracy in Action features throughout the book and try to answer the questions that accompany some of them.

An Ancient Start

Today, democracy is a widespread system of government around the world. Most countries have some form of democracy, and democracy is certainly not a new idea. From the earliest times, some societies tried to include at least some part of the population in deciding how their community should be run. Over many centuries, this style of government has spread across the globe and become very popular.

Ruled by One Leader

For centuries, states were ruled by a single, powerful leader. He, or sometimes she, was a king, queen, emperor, or even a dictator. The ruler seized power, inherited it, or gained it because they were part of an elite group, such as a landowner or a military leader. However, these rulers couldn't govern entirely alone. They often set up institutions to help them govern, and these institutions represented the interests of at least some of the people. Sometimes, institutions grew in power, especially if the ruler needed their support. They gradually increased their control over the ruler's behavior. In some cases, the institutions came to represent more and more of the people. They gained enough power to share the running of the country with the ruler, and for their countries to become more democratic.

Henry VIII of England (1491–1547) was a powerful king, but he also relied on his advisors to help him rule.

A Changing System

The idea of who "the people" are has changed a great deal over time. Early democracies would not seem very democratic to us today, as the definition of a "citizen" was limited to a small part of the male population. Women were excluded from politics for many years and have only in recent history been given the vote. Gradually, the right to vote was then extended to more groups in society.

Democracy in Action

One modern-day example of direct democracy in action is a referendum. This is a vote by all the people on a particular issue. Governments may hold a referendum on an issue that is especially important for a nation's future. For example, in 2016 the United Kingdom (UK) held a referendum on whether to stay in the EU or leave it. The outcome of the vote was to leave.

The result of the EU referendum has caused great division in the UK, do you think it was right to allow the referendum based on the values of democracy?

Today, a true democracy includes all walks of life—whatever a person's gender, religion, race, or status.

PAST AND PRESENT:

If the referendum was held again in the near future, do you think the outcome would be the same? Give reasons for your answer.

An Age-Old System

Democracy appeared for the first time thousands of years ago, in ancient Greece. The country then consisted of a group of city-states. Each was independent, with a strong capital city. Some of the best-known city-states were Athens, Sparta, Thebes, and Corinth. The strongest was Athens, which is now considered to be the birthplace of democracy.

The Home of Democracy

Athens was the home of the first democracy, in the fifth century BCE. It was a direct democracy. Its citizens met together in the assembly to vote on laws and other issues, such as going to war. They also elected their own leader. Men who had completed two years of military service were citizens, whatever their wealth. Women were excluded, however, and so were foreigners and slaves. Everyday matters were decided in a Council of Five Hundred, whose members were all men who had been chosen by lot. This was a system of randomly choosing people to prevent individuals from gaining control of the Council and influencing it.

The Roman Empire saw both democracy and rule by one leader. When the military leader Julius Caesar (100–44 BCE) took power, he made himself emperor. For 400 years after the event, the Roman Empire was ruled by an emperor and democracy was put on hold.

Change Elsewhere

For centuries, ancient Rome in Italy was governed as a republic. It was not a democracy, but it had some democratic elements. The two leaders, the consuls, were elected every year. Their power was controlled by the senate, a group of wealthy citizens who ruled for life. All citizens could serve in the assembly, which voted on certain laws and issues of war and peace. This system continued for hundreds of years until dramatic change came with the use of military force. In 45 BCE, the military leader Julius Caesar took hold of power for himself and ancient Rome became an empire that dominated much of the world.

PEOPLE AND POLITICS

Two of the greatest philosophers of ancient Greece were not in favor of democracy. Plato (c.427–347 BCE) thought that governing should be carried out only by men who had the right training and skills.

Aristotle (384–322 BCE) thought that democracy was an unstable system, because powerful individuals could influence the assembly, to make them vote unwisely. Aristotle believed government should be by the wealthy, who do not need to work and have time for political duties.

Pericles was the leader of Athens from about 460 to 429 BCE, when the city-state was at its height. In contrast to Aristotle and Plato, Pericles was a strong supporter of democracy. He restricted the powers of the unelected council, and he brought reforms to the legal system.

Pericles, Aristotle, and Plato had differing views on how societies should be governed. This image shows Plato and Aristotle arguing.

Having Little Say

After the end of the Roman Empire, Europe split into a collection of small nations, ruled by powerful individuals. For 600 years, society was strictly hierarchical. The king was at the top, with the clergy, lords and landowners in the middle, and the peasant farmers at the bottom. Very few people had any say in how their country was governed.

Many Years in the Making

Some of the institutions of democracy did begin to develop during medieval times, however. In the 900s, in Iceland, an assembly of chiefs called the Althing met to vote on laws and settle arguments. This gathering has been called the first parliament in Europe. In other countries, the king would gather a council of the most powerful lords, to advise him and approve the taxes he wanted to raise. Over time, these assemblies came to represent not just the nobility but also the clergy, and the people. These powerful groups of people became known as the Three Estates, and they could voice their grievances at an assembly.

A Parliament

In England from the 1200s, the representative assembly was called parliament. Parliament grew in power over the centuries, and became the source of new laws. Although England saw a shift in power in which government gained more control, this change did not happen all over Europe. In many European countries, monarchs ruled with more absolute power and democracy was stalled. Things changed in 1689, when the English parliament forced the king to sign the Declaration of Rights. This established the democratic principles of free, fair, and frequent elections, and freedom of speech in parliament.

The Magna Carta

The Magna Carta—which means Great Charter—of 1215 is one of the founding documents of democracy. The Charter limited the power of King John of England (1166–1216) by stating that he could not raise taxes without the barons' permission. Nor could the king imprison people at will.

The principle of the Magna Carta was that the law must be freely available to all, no matter their social status. It was vital in the development of democracy.

PEOPLE AND POLITICS

The barons of King John forced him to sign the Magna Carta because he had ruled unwisely. The image below shows King John protesting the signing of the Magna Carta, which reduced his powers.

The barons created the Magna Carta to try and control the range of power a king had, because of issues that had arisen during King John's reign. Battles with France had resulted in the loss of a lot of land. They had also cost the country a great deal of money, with the barons paying the most in taxes. The barons wanted to protect people's lives, property, and right to justice. A council of 25 barons was formed to watch over the king. They would later become England's Parliament. John died in 1216 and was succeeded by his son, Henry III. The Magna Carta was then changed and amended, with a final version being agreed and signed with the barons in 1225.

Change in America

In the eighteenth century, the British tradition of parliament extended to the 13 colonies in North America. These communities had their own assemblies, and some control over their government. Before long, they began to resent Britain's demand for taxes. They thought these payments to a faraway country were unfair. Life in North America was about to change in a dramatic way.

A New Constitution

The colonists complained about paying taxes to Britain when they had no representation in the British parliament. Then, in 1775, a series of rebellions started in North America. These revolts became known as the American Revolution. Britain responded by sending more troops across the Atlantic to try to restore law and order. However, in the decade that followed, Britain began to lose its grip on government in North America. Finally, in 1783, the British accepted that America would become a new, separate country. A new constitution was drafted for the United States of America (USA).

After nearly eight years of war, the British surrendered in 1781 and left the former colonies of North America.

The World's Most Powerful Democracy

The newly founded USA was a nation made up of a federation of states. Each state retained its own government and laws, serving the particular needs of its citizens. The federal (national) government made laws of national importance. The new constitution was based on democratic principles, and ensured that no branch of the federal government could become too powerful. It was the beginnings of a new system of government for North America and the founding of what is still considered the world's most powerful democratic nation.

Democracy in Action

In 1776, one of the leaders of the colonists, Thomas Jefferson, wrote the Declaration of Independence. Its opening words are: "We hold these truths to be self-evident, that all men are created equal, that they are endowed by their Creator with certain unalienable Rights, that among these are Life, Liberty, and the pursuit of Happiness." Government, he says, exists for the good of the people, and takes its power from the people.

What do you think Jefferson is saying about the rights of the individual?

PAST AND PRESENT:

Do you think the opening words of the Declaration of Independence are respected in the United States today? Give reasons for your answer.

This famous painting depicts the Declaration of Independence, when the 13 North American British colonies separated from British rule in 1776.

A Growing Authority

During the 1700s in Britain, the authority of parliament grew. The monarch needed parliament's support to govern. Members of parliament divided loosely into political parties, and the idea of a chief minister supported by the biggest party—the prime minister—evolved. Over the next 200 years, almost all western European countries, along with the United States, Canada, Australia, and New Zealand, developed their own democratic systems.

The French Revolution

One important and far-reaching influence on democracy was the French Revolution. In the late 1700s, radicals in France overthrew the monarch and passed a Declaration of Rights that stated that "The source of all sovereignty resides essentially in the nation." After centuries of rule by kings, the ordinary people of France began to take power and the governance of their country into their own hands. In Britain too, a series of Reform Acts in the 1800s extended the franchise, or right to vote, to many more people. Both Germany and France gave all men the franchise.

The Blot of Slavery

In the United States, all adult white men had the right to vote by the mid-1800s. However, the existence of slavery in the southern states was a blot on this democratic progress. The North called for its abolition, and the Civil War that followed in 1861–1865 resulted in the defeat of the South, the abolition of slavery, and the extension of the franchise to Black men. It would take another century, however, for Black people to achieve complete political equality.

This illustration shows revolutionaries storming the Bastille prison in Paris, France, in 1789.

PEOPLE AND POLITICS

Abraham Lincoln was the sixteenth president of the United States. He opposed slavery and after his election, a number of southern states began to withdraw from the Union of the United States, leading to civil war. Although the Unionists eventually won the war, Abraham Lincoln was assassinated a few days later.

Abraham Lincoln led the United States through the American Civil War, defending the nation and abolishing slavery.

Democracy in Action

Another, more peaceful revolution affected the development of democracy. The Industrial Revolution (1760–1840), which began in Britain, brought great technological developments and changed societies forever. It created a wealthy middle class of industrialists, and the working class moved from the land to factories and cities.

Why do you think the Industrial Revolution had an impact on democracy?

New Challenges

During the twentieth century, democracy faced many challenges from more absolute, authoritarian forms of government. However, by 2000, democracy had been adopted in many parts of world. The steady progress of democracy, spanning hundreds of years, meant this type of government became widely accepted as the most desirable choice. Today, it is still the case that democracy is the most-favored political system, with many countries employing it.

The Turmoil of War

After the great political turmoil and widespread devastation caused by World War I (1914–1918), many states committed to democracy. Ordinary men and women could vote, and political parties grew up to represent their interests. Socialists, for example, argued for a more equal distribution of wealth in society, to give a better standard of living to the poorest. They thought that political equality was of little use unless there was economic equality, too.

PEOPLE AND POLITICS

When Germany's fascist leader, Adolf Hitler (1889–1945), invaded neighboring countries, his actions led to World War II (1939–1945), one of the most devastating wars the world has ever seen. The Italian leader Benito Mussolini (1883–1945) joined the fight, leading his country into conflict under the rule of his fascist government. The defeat of Germany and Italy in World War II brought an end to fascist rule in both countries. Hitler and Mussolini have since become synonymous with the term "fascist."

Adolf Hitler

The Rise of Fascism

One political system that posed a threat to democracy, however, was fascism. This system favored strong, centralized government and banned all forms of opposition. Fascist governments took control in Germany, Italy, and Spain in the 1920s and 1930s and facism became a powerful political force in Europe.

Democracy in Action

During World War II, the US government produced persuasive propaganda, such as posters showing a "two-headed monster of the Germans and the Japanese," and urging people to work hard in factories to produce goods to support the war effort.

What messages do you think such posters were intended to give?

PAST AND PRESENT:

Do you think a similar campaign of propaganda would work in modern democracies today? How do you think such a campaign would be run, for example, by social media?

The Challenge of Communism

Another challenge to democracy came from a political system called communism, in the Soviet Union and elsewhere. In this extreme form of socialism, the state controlled all wealth, to give a better standard of living to the poorest people. However, to achieve these goals, a single party governed with absolute authority. As a result, the people had no say, and most continued to live in poverty with living standards very poor throughout much of the Union.

In the 1980s, the Soviet Union began to open up the economy and reduce state control of it. That allowed businesses and industry to function in a way more similar to that of democratic economies. The Soviet government believed that this new flourishing economy would encourage a renewed commitment to communism. However, it had the opposite effect and people began to reject the political system. As communism began to fail, the Soviet Union broke up in 1991, and democracy gradually emerged.

CHAPTER 2

Understanding Democracy

Democracies vary in detail around the world, but all are representative democracies at national level. Elected representatives create and vote on laws, and they also make decisions about how their country should be run. However, the basis of the representatives' power lies with ordinary people. The representatives can be voted out of office at the next election if the people do not approve of their policies.

Rules and Principles

A constitution is a set of rules and principles that lays down how a nation should be governed. This fundamental document places limits on the power of government, and guarantees the political rights and freedom of individuals, even against the majority. Most countries, such as the United States, have a written constitution. It has been added to, or amended, many times since it was first written in 1787. The UK, on the other hand, does not. Its "unwritten constitution" is determined by its historical customs, laws, and habits.

Three Branches

There are three branches of government in a democracy, but the ways in which they work together vary in different countries. They are: the executive branch, which creates policies and carries them out; the legislature, which debates and approves the laws proposed by the executive branch; and the judiciary, or the courts and judges. The judiciary decide whether laws have been broken, and settle any arguments about interpretations of the law when they arise.

The division of power between these key three branches is called the Separation of Powers. The basic principle of the Separation of Powers ensures that the three branches of government remain independent of each other, to prevent any one of them becoming too powerful and exerting too much influence over a country. That ensures the system of democracy functions without any one person or group gaining a dangerous amount of control.

Critics of democracy suggest that giving power to all the people can lead to bad government. The famous English playwright George Bernard Shaw said, "Democracy substitutes election by the incompetent many for appointment by the corrupt few."

President Franklin D. Roosevelt (1882–1945) said, "Democracy cannot succeed unless those who express their choice are prepared to choose wisely. The real safeguard of democracy, therefore, is education." Roosevelt led the United States through the Great Depression of the 1930s and through World War II. The policies of his "New Deal" helped to stabilize the economy and improve the lives of the poorest people.

Sir Winston Churchill (1874–1965) who served twice as the British prime minister said, "The best argument against democracy is a five-minute conversation with the average voter." Churchill was an inspirational leader who rallied the British people during World War II and led his country from the brink of defeat to victory.

Franklin D. Roosevelt

Sir Winston Churchill

The president lives and works in the White House in Washington, D.C. This is also where he meets with the cabinet.

Daily Responsibilities

In a democracy, the executive branch is responsible for the day-to-day running of the country. It makes policy and puts it into action. It is sometimes called "the government." This part of a political system is most closely linked to ordinary people. It tries to keep up with public opinion, while also working to create policies that are affordable, achievable, and in the best interests of the people who are affected by the policies.

Elected Politicians

The members of the executive branch are elected politicians. They are often called ministers, and each one has responsibility for a particular area of government, such as health, social care, education, or foreign affairs. In the United States, the minister responsible for foreign affairs is called the Secretary of State, while in Britain they are called the Foreign Secretary. Members of the executive branch meet as a group, in cabinet, to discuss their decisions and make policy. The members of the executive branch do not make the laws, but they do put forward ideas about how laws could be created or changed. The executive branch is led by the chief executive. This person has different names in different countries. In the United States that person is the president.

Who Is in Charge?

Britain has a prime minister as its chief executive and Germany has a chancellor. In 2021, Olaf Scholz was elected Chancellor, succeeding Angela Merkel, the first woman ever to hold this office in Germany. Scholz leads a coalition of several political parties in the country's government and is a powerful figure within the European Union (EU), too. In a presidential system, the chief executive is also the Head of State.

Democracy in Action

The government employs a large group of people to put their policies into effect. They are public servants, or civil servants. These people are not elected, instead, they are professionals in the public administration. They develop expertise in their chosen area of policy during their careers, and also figure out how changes will happen.

Can you think how civil servants could influence the extent to which new policies come into effect? Is this democratic?

In Britain, the monarch is the Head of State, and the prime minister is the leader of the largest political party in the legislature, or parliament. King Charles is Britain's current Head of State.

Making Laws

The legislature makes laws. It is made up of elected representatives of the people and is often called a parliament, assembly, or congress. The legislature acts as a check on the executive branch, by debating its proposals and deciding which should become law. The judiciary is the system of courts and judges that carries out justice. It interprets laws made by the legislature, and acts to protect the rights of citizens. The way that the legislature functions is clearly set out in the Constitution.

Kept Separate

In the United States, the legislative assembly and the executive branch are kept separate. The president is not a member, but is elected in a separate presidential election.

In a parliamentary system, such as in the UK, Germany, and India, there is one election for both bodies. The executive branch members sit in the legislature, and are drawn from the political party with the most seats in the assembly. The legislature often consists of two assemblies.

The Supreme Court in Washington, D.C., is the highest court in the federal judiciary of the United States.

How the System Works

In the United States, congress is made up of two bodies: the House of Representatives and the Senate. Both are elected. Members of the House of Representatives are elected every two years. In the UK, parliament consists of two bodies also: the House of Commons and the House of Lords. The lords are appointed, not elected.

In both the US and UK systems, there are two chambers to spread power and decision making, so that one group is kept in check by the other. In both instances, the second chamber—such as the House of Lords or the House of Representatives—acts as a brake to hold back any hasty decisions from the first chamber—such as the House of Commons or the Senate.

A System of Courts

The judiciary consists of a system of courts, starting with smaller, local ones, and ending with a supreme court. This is the ultimate decision maker and the court of final appeal. State courts try most of the cases that come to law. However, extreme or controversial cases are often taken to the supreme court for special attention and to decide an outcome.

Democracy in Action

One feature of the judicial system in a democracy is "trial by jury." When certain cases come to court, the outcome is decided by a jury of ordinary citizens, chosen at random from the population. They hear the arguments for and against in a case, and decide if the person is guilty or innocent. Usually, everyone on the jury must decide the same way for a decision to be valid. This is called a unanimous decision.

Do you think trial by jury is a fair or effective system?

Do you believe the jurors should be impartial, or neutral, in their thinking?

PAST AND PRESENT:

Do you think our current system of judge and jury will continue? Do you think it could be replaced? If so, by what?

The Will of the People

Democracies represent the will of the people. That means the purpose of democracies is to make sure that what the majority of people in a country want to happen does, in fact, happen. However, people have different views on how they want their country to be run. Their representatives therefore organize themselves into rival groups, or political parties. In a democracy, people choose which party to support. The way to decide which party has the greatest control over decision making is to hold elections.

The Choice for Voters

Political parties set out the choice for voters in elections. Some parties, such as the US Democratic Party, represent a wide range of views on many issues. Others, such as the Green Party, are more focused in their objectives. The party that has the most representatives elected to the legislature is in control of policy-making, until the next election. In some countries, such as Germany, many parties win seats and they form a coalition to govern. In others, such as the United States, there are only two main parties and one wins a clear majority. This produces stronger, more stable government, but the minority views have less influence.

Politicians work hard to campaign before elections to convince the public that they should vote for a particular political party.

A Right to Vote

The right to vote in elections is known as suffrage. During the nineteenth century, the vote was gradually extended to more groups in society. Women were one of the last groups to win this right. Women achieved suffrage first in New Zealand in 1893. The United States followed in 1920 and Britain in 1928. Women campaigned hard for the right, and some were injured or even killed during protests.

"The Suffragette," June 13, 1913.

Registered at the G.P.O. as a Newspaper

The Suffragette

The Official Organ of the Women's Social and Political Union

Edited by Christabel Pankhurst.

FRIDAY, JUNE 13, 1913.

Price 1d. Weekly (Post Free 1½d.)

No. 35—Vol. 1.

IN HONOUR AND IN LOVING, REVERENT MEMORY OF

EMILY WILDING DAVISON.

SHE DIED FOR WOMEN.

"Greater love hath no man than this, that he lay down his life for his friends."

Miss Davison, who made a protest at the Derby against the denial of Votes to Women, was knocked down by the King's horse and sustained terrible injuries of which she died on Sunday, June 8th, 1913.

Democracy in Action

The cover of a magazine for suffrage supporters in Britain showed one protester, Emily Davison, who died in a protest in 1913. She was killed when she threw herself under the king's horse at a race called the Derby in protest at the government's failure to give women the right to vote. Emily had used violence in her previous campaigns, and had been to prison. However, on the cover of the magazine she was portrayed as an angel, who had "died for women."

PAST AND PRESENT:

Can you think of a scenario in which violent protest might be portrayed as heroic in a modern democracy? Can you provide examples of recent events in which this may have been the case?

Emily Davison lost her life in the campaign for women's voting rights in Britain.

CHAPTER 3

Life in a Democracy

In the modern world, nearly all the most powerful states are multiparty democracies. In most of the monarchies around the world, real power rests not with the monarch but with the three branches of government. There remain, however, some dictatorships. In these political systems, one leader exercises absolute power and imposes great restraints on people's freedom. However, the pressure for these countries to move toward democracy is increasing.

Elected to Serve

In a democracy, the people elect the government to fulfil basic functions. These include defending the country from harm or invasion, providing effective services such as health, education, roads, and utilities (such as water, gas, and electricity), and providing a support system for those most in need in society. People put their faith in elected politicians, and expect them to fulfil the promises they made when they were voted into office. This faith keeps a democracy working smoothly, without people feeling the need to protest or cause a rebellion.

Government services keep a country running smoothly, and people vote for politicians to represent their interests.

Unrest broke out on the streets of Buenos Aires in 2019 as people protested in opposition to their government.

People Power

From time to time, citizens feel compelled to rebel against their government. The way a government responds to these challenges is crucial for democracy to be upheld. In 2019, for example, people took to the streets of Buenos Aires, Argentina, demanding far more government action to help the poor. In presidential elections that took place a month later, people voted overwhelmingly for policies that put the economy first.

Responsibilities for All

In return for good government, the people have responsibilities, too. They must behave responsibly toward others to create a safe and happy society, they must obey the law, and they must try to be informed when they use their vote. A democracy only works effectively if the people in it understand the political choices presented to them, and use their vote wisely to elect a good representative government. The politicians keep a democracy running on a day-to-day basis, but the people need to play an active role, too.

Democracy in Action

In a democracy, people are elected to hold office in government for a limited time only. This is a good thing in one way, because it prevents the total control of power by any one party. However, it can also mean that governments make policy for the short term, in order to get reelected. They may focus on winning the next election, rather than working for the long-term interests of the country. Terms of office often run for a number of years.

Do you think terms of office that run for a number of years are good or bad? Give reasons for your answer.

The Rule of Law

The principle of the rule of law is fundamental to the system of democracy. It means that everyone should know the law, and that the law should apply to everyone equally. Everyone, whatever their gender, race, religion, or status, must act within the law and the constitution.

In return for its citizens living by the rule of law, a government must in turn uphold the law. By doing so, the government will encourage citizens to continue to live law-abiding lives. Those combined efforts provide a safe and stable community for everyone in a democracy to live in.

A Strong Constitution

For the rule of law to work effectively, a country must have strong, rigorous institutions. Everyone must know that the judiciary is well organized, well trained, and impartial, or without bias. They must know that public officials and institutions, at all levels in society, even the highest, can be challenged if they appear to be acting outside the law. Citizens will feel safe if they know that all arguments will be settled peacefully, and that effective action and punishment is available if they suffer harm from someone who acts against the law. If people know the law works, they are much more likely to obey it.

The police work on behalf of a government to uphold the law and to keep citizens safe and secure.

Protecting the People

The rule of law also exists to protect people from a government that tries to abuse the powers it has been given. One of the roles of the United Nations (UN) is to protect the principle of the rule of law around the world. The UN is an international organization with 193 member countries. It was founded in 1945, after World War II, to promote world peace, and improve living conditions and human rights for people everywhere. The UN works to develop an international standard for the rule of law in many countries, especially those either experiencing wars or having recently ended them. This can be an important step on the road to creating or improving democracy in those countries.

PEOPLE AND POLITICS

"Man's capacity for justice makes democracy possible, but man's inclination to injustice makes democracy necessary." This was said by Reinhold Niebuhr (1892–1971) in 1944. Niebuhr was a religious and political thinker. One of his theories was that sin was a part of human nature. He said that although individuals could sometimes put their self-interest to one side in favor of the greater good, the actions of groups of individuals, like nations, were governed by self-interest. And therefore, groups in society made individuals worse.

The UN headquarters in New York City displays the flags of all member states.

Political Rights for All

Another fundamental principle of democracy is that all adults have the same political rights, regardless of their gender, age, race, or religious belief. In a democracy, the belief is that all people should be treated equally, whatever their situation. In a democracy, all citizens have a right to a safe and free life. Even those who cannot vote, such as children, are protected by the law.

The Question of Race

In the United States, democracy was denied to Black people in the South until the 1960s. Although the Constitution upheld the right of all people to vote, Blacks were denied suffrage in some states and forced to live separately, as second-class citizens. The Civil Rights Movement, led by Martin Luther King Jr. (1929–1968), grew up in protest at this. Federal laws were finally passed to ensure there was political equality throughout the country. In South Africa, a similar situation existed. The white minority dominated the country, and nonwhite South Africans had few rights. The first multiracial election in South Africa, based on universal suffrage, finally took place in 1994. It was a landmark moment.

The Question of Gender

We have seen that women had to fight harder than men to gain the right to vote in national elections.

Martin Luther King Jr.

Since then, many democracies have passed legislation that also protects the rights of men and women to equal opportunity and treatment, in the workplace and elsewhere. Laws also protect against discrimination on the grounds of age and religious belief. Children are also protected by laws. Although the voting age is 18 in many democracies, adults there have passed laws on behalf of children to ensure their safety and wellbeing.

Democracy in Action

In 1948, the UN adopted the Universal Declaration of Human Rights. This document lays out the basic rights that all humans should have, anywhere in the world. Humans are free, and entitled to rights without gender, race, religious, or wealth discrimination. Their rights include equal treatment under the law, privacy at home, freedom to travel, to own property, to take part in government, to work, to education, to adequate living standards, and to express an opinion. These rights underpin all democracies.

Why do you think the Universal Declaration of Human Rights was drawn up shortly after the end of World War II?

PAST AND PRESENT: Do you believe the document is still relevant today? Do you think it is honored in modern democracies such as that of the United States?

In a democracy, all people should be treated equally regardless of their age, gender, race, religion, or other differences.

The Right of Freedom

The freedom to express an opinion, and to seek and receive information, is another important principle of democracy. People can say what they think of the government without fear of being arrested, as long as they do not break laws. In a democracy, it is usually against the law to encourage hatred or violence in other people, on grounds of religion or other factors.

What People Think and Want

A government must know what people think and want to be able to respond to their needs. Individuals can speak out alone, but in complex societies the media has the most powerful voice in expressing different opinions. Newspapers, broadcasters, and Internet media are powerful forces in a democracy. They can investigate and expose wrongdoing in government. For example, American journalists exposed the wrongdoing of President Nixon in the Watergate scandal, forcing him to resign in 1974. More recently, Donald Trump has also been in the news because of allegations made about his actions before and during his presidency.

PEOPLE AND POLITICS

In 1974, Richard Nixon (1913–1994) became the only US president to resign. Two years earlier, five men had been arrested trying to bug the offices of the Democratic Party in Washington, D.C., during the presidential election campaign. Nixon tried to cover up any involvement in the scandal but was forced to resign when growing evidence put his administration at fault.

Richard Nixon

Influenced by the Media

The media can also influence public opinion. Coverage of all news stories can be biased, but in important events, such as a decision to go to war, or in a general election, a journalist's choice of which side to support can make a huge difference. People can be influenced by the opinions they read or hear. Media reports have the power to reinforce someone's own beliefs, or to persuade them to make a particular judgment.

The media holds a lot of power when it comes to influencing people's political decisions. For that reason, politicians try to maintain a close relationship with the media.

Newspapers and other media forms are commercial businesses. Along with wanting to tell the truth and encourage debate, they need to sell newspapers, or attract the most viewers, to make a profit. Some people say this has made them trivialize or simplify the issues, and concentrate more on the personalities of people in public life, rather than their policies. They have been invading people's privacy to get at a "sensational" story.

What do you think? Has the media lost its way as an effective check on government?

CHAPTER 4

The Struggle for Democracy

Many countries around the world are engaged in a struggle to achieve a more democratic government. For some of these countries, decades of dictatorships have left the people powerless, and fighting for democracy is a challenging task. Other countries are facing serious poverty. When day-to-day life is a struggle for food, water, and shelter, it's very difficult for people to find the energy to take part in political decisions.

The African Union headquarters in Addis Ababa, Ethiopia, gathers the leaders of African nations together to work toward a more peaceful and prosperous future.

A Fight for Independence

In the second half of the twentieth century, the countries of Africa that had been colonies of European countries gained their independence. Although parliamentary regimes were often set up, few survived. Powerful individuals established dictatorships, or the military seized control. Civil wars followed in many countries.

Stable, democratic government is still not widespread in Africa, mainly because there is so much poverty. People's main concerns are about food, shelter, and work, rather than political freedom, and many receive little education. In 2002, the African Union was formed to help improve the continent's democracy, human rights, and economy, by bringing an end to conflicts and promoting cooperation. Since 2017, all African countries have become members of the African Union, although some have been suspended in recent years for their involvement in military coups and acts of violence.

The Arab Spring

In late 2010 and 2011, in North Africa and the Middle East, a series of protests began against the undemocratic governments of several countries. Together, they are known as "The Arab Spring." They began in Tunisia, and spread to Libya, Jordan, Egypt, Syria, and elsewhere. Although the Tunisian government fell and the country went on to build a democracy, a decade of slow economic growth has led to more authoritarian measures there again. Meanwhile, dictators in other countries vowed to rule with an even tighter fist.

Democracy in Action

In Syria, the protests that began with the Arab Spring turned into a terrible civil war that has been raging for over a decade. More than half a million people have lost their lives and at least 12 million are either internally displaced or living as refugees abroad. The authoritarian government led by President Assad continues to rule relentlessly.

Western countries have been reluctant to intervene with military force to stop the bloodshed in Syria. Do you think they should intervene, or should the region be left to deal with its problems?

The ongoing civil war in Syria has destroyed entire neighborhoods, disrupted people's lives, and put children's education on hold.

Fighting for Freedom

In 2022, Russia launched a full-scale invasion of Ukraine, which would become the biggest war in Europe since World War II. Within two years, at least 10,000 civilians had been killed, and more than 14 million civilians have needed humanitarian aid. Four million had left their homes within the country, while more than 6 million had fled the country itself, to live abroad as refugees.

Disputed Land

Ukraine lies at the crossroads of Europe and Russia. In 1922, it was one of the founding members of the Soviet Union but later gained independence when the Soviet Union collapsed in 1991. Despite the country's independence, Russia still sees Ukraine as part of its own country. In the 1950s, Russia gifted Crimea to Ukraine while it was part of the Soviet Union, but when Ukraine gained independence, Russia wanted this land back. Tensions resurfaced in 2014, when Russia invaded Crimea and took back control of the region.

Extensive damage to a residential apartment block in the Ukrainian capital, Kyiv, attacked by Russian aircraft.

PEOPLE AND POLITICS

Vladimir Putin has been president of Russia since 2012 but has held continuous positions of president or prime minister since 1999. This means he has been in power for one-quarter of a century. When Putin first came to power, Russian presidents ruled for no more than two consecutive terms of six years. But in 2020, Putin amended the constitution so he could remain president for two more terms, potentially staying in office until 2036.

Growing Tensions

Before the invasion of Crimea in 2014, there were tensions in Ukraine between those who favored further integration with the EU, and those who felt more closely tied to Russia. In 2004, former Ukrainian president Viktor Yushchenko was poisoned and almost killed while running for presidency. Yushchenko favored democracy and closer ties with Europe, while his opponents were drawn toward Russia. Yushchenko survived his assassination attempt and went on to serve as president from 2005–2010.

Democracy in Action

The Russian invasion of Ukraine in 2022 was an escalation of the Russo-Ukrainian war that started with the invasion of Crimea almost a decade earlier. In 2014 and 2015, in a bid to end the conflict, France and Germany oversaw a series of negotiations between Russia and Ukraine, known as the Minsk agreements. However, both sides had different views on how the terms should be implemented and by the time Russia invaded in February 2022, the agreements were effectively dead.

Do you think the West should have done more to negotiate peace between Ukraine and Russia after the invasion of Crimea? What difficulties might get in the way of any peace negotiations?

The American Dream

Democracy is a developed system of government that needs constant checks and balances to ensure that it remains free and fair to all. Even in the most democratic of nations, external challenges can put democracy under threat. In recent years, the United States has been one example of a nation grappling with its democratic principles.

Freedom for All

The American Dream is an ideal in US society, entrenched in democracy. It's a view that with universal rights and freedoms, anyone can succeed in life, according to their abilities or achievement through hard work, whatever that person's background. But despite these democratic claims, universal rights aren't always upheld.

Voting Restrictions

In a democratic nation, all adult citizens have the right to vote and their engagement in the political process is crucial for democracy to flourish. In recent years, however, there has been restricted access to the ballot box. This includes limited voting times, compulsory voter ID, and restricted voter registration —all practices that affect minority groups, the poor, the young, and the elderly. At the same time, voter fraud (such as people using a false name or coercing others to vote a particular way) has been influencing and damaging the democratic process.

Voter identification can help to prevent voter fraud, but some minority groups are unable to get an ID card.

Loss of Trust

When democracy fails, there can be a loss of trust in the government. In 2020, Donald Trump claimed election fraud had cost him the presidential election—and even when these claims were checked and refuted, a seed of doubt remained in many voters' minds. If a country wants a secure and stable environment in which it can prosper, it needs the confidence and backing of its citizens. Without that, democracy is impossible.

The Problem of Misinformation

The success of democracy also comes from citizens believing reliable information. During the Trump administration, conspiracy theories about the COVID-19 pandemic meant many people lost trust in the government, and lost confidence in what to believe. Trump's assertion of election fraud also gained momentum. In a survey in January 2021, three-quarters of Trump supporters believed Trump was "definitely or probably" the rightful winner of the presidential election, despite courts around the country rejecting these claims and all US states certifying their results.

PEOPLE AND POLITICS

In 2021, more than 2,000 rioters stormed the Capitol Building in Washington, D.C. in support of Donald Trump who had lost the presidential election. They were trying to disrupt the formal declaration of Joe Biden as president, to keep Trump in power. Although Trump was later cleared of charges, he was accused of encouraging the rebellion.

Rioters clashed with police as they tried to enter the Capitol Building in Washington, D.C., in 2021.

CHAPTER 5

The Future of Democracy

Today, all the world's most powerful states have a democratic government, apart from China. Many other countries are striving for it too. However, democracy, though popular, also faces some great challenges. In some established democracies, governments are struggling to keep their citizens involved in the political process. Others are facing the challenge of upholding people's freedom against the rule of law.

Democracy in the West

In western countries that have enjoyed democracy for a long time, people have become less interested in politics, and play a less-active part in their democracy. In fact, many people never vote in elections because they have little trust in the will of their politicians to represent their views, and think they have little or no chance of influencing policy. Political parties in the United States and Europe are funded by big business or wealthy individuals, who, in turn may influence policy and pay for lavish election campaigns. It would be dangerous, however, to take our democracy for granted.

PEOPLE AND POLITICS

In 2018, a number of high-profile Spanish politicians and businessmen were convicted of fraud in Spain's worst-ever political corruption scandal. The case involved businessmen, such as Francisco Correa Sánchez, who had bribed Spanish politicians with money to gain government contracts. Shortly after the convictions, Spain's prime minister Mariano Rajoy announced his resignation when he was ousted from position by a vote of no confidence.

Mariano Rajoy

A Growing Awareness

There is a growing international recognition of the importance of human rights, and that these rights are best preserved in a democracy. For the newly developing economies of the world to establish successful democracies, they need to ensure three things. First, that there are honest and committed individuals to hold office in government; second, that enough people are educated to serve in the public administration; and, third, that the judiciary, the media, and other institutions can act as powerful, independent checks on the government.

Democracy in Action

The problem of terrorism poses a challenge to democracies today. Terrorists use violence against innocent people to promote their political ideas and to achieve their goals. They put pressure on governments and the fear of terrorism can influence political views.

How should governments deal with the threat of terrorism, and still maintain the rule of law and human rights?

If there is clear evidence against terrorists, they can be tried using the law. But what about people suspected of plotting terrorist acts? Should they be imprisoned without trial, to prevent them from acting? This may be a breach of their liberty, but is it justifiable because of the greater threat to the safety of the population? What do you think?

Candles and flowers were placed in memory of the people killed during a terrorist attack in Israel in 2022. Governments faced with terrorism are in a difficult position —trying to protect citizens from both the demands and the threats of terrorists.

The Might of China

China is the world's second-largest economy, but it remains a communist country. In 1989, a protest movement in favor of democracy was violently suppressed by the government. The Communist Party has absolute power and still cracks down on any opposition. In a world where most countries give citizens a voice, can or will this economic superpower move to a more democratic government? There are divided opinions about whether this is or is not possible.

Solving Problems

Despite its economic success, China faces many problems. Millions of people live in poverty and receive little education, and an ever-aging population needs more and more healthcare. Industrial development has also created dangerously high levels of air pollution. The Chinese government is putting its energy into solving these economic and social problems, with the control that authoritarian rule brings. But many people have criticized that authoritarian rule and the effect

The National People's Congress of China (NPC) meets only once a year and has very few powers. It merely approves all the decisions of the Communist Party, which is headed by Xi Jinping (below). The leader has controlled China since 2013.

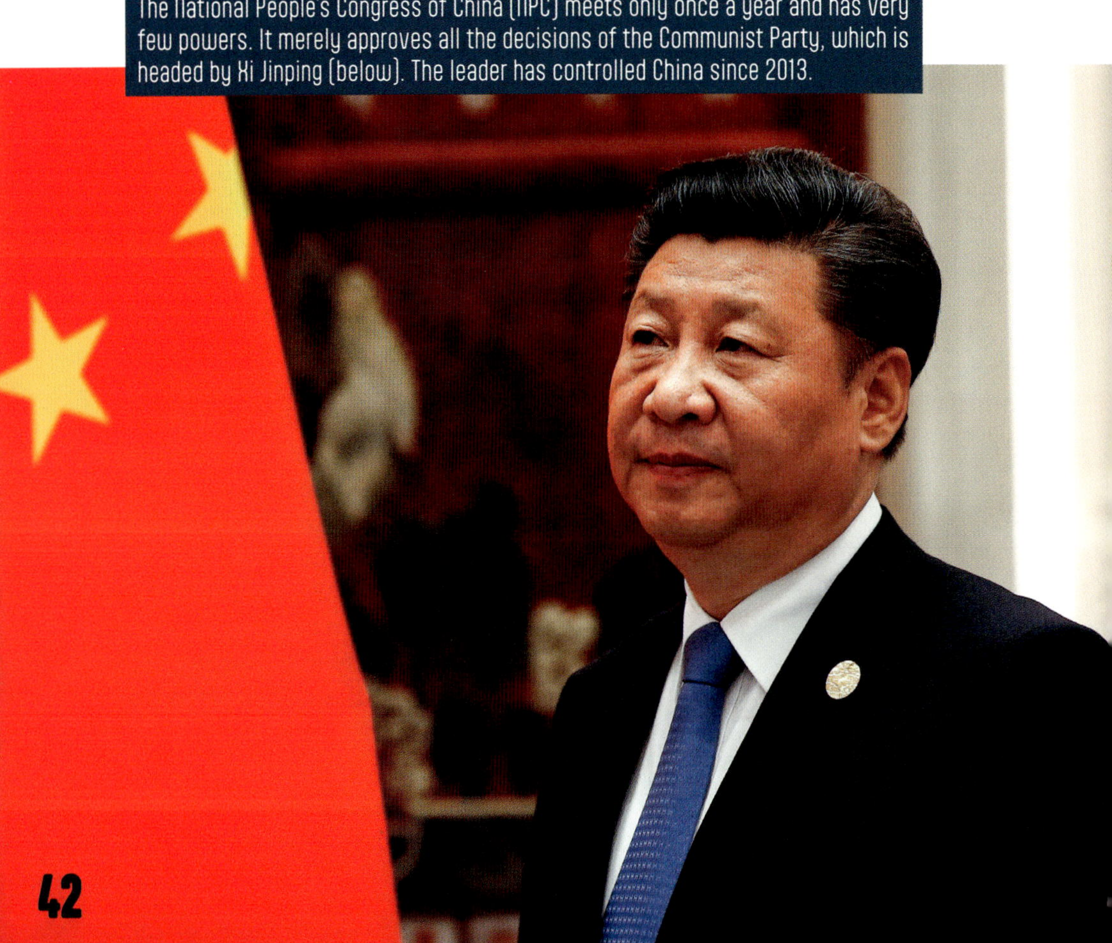

that government by absolute power has had on the people of China. They claim that the government has not addressed many of the needs of Chinese people and had neglected their basic human rights, resulting in hardship for many citizens.

A New Direction

In 2013, the new leaders of the Communist Party took office. They continued the country's long history of authoritarian rule, but with new policies that sought to make China prosperous and proud again. After years of corruption in government, President Xi Jinping carried out an anti-corruption drive to restore public respect for the Party and sought to reduce inequalities in wealth. He has talked of democratic principles, such as fairness, justice, security and a better environment, with the aim of giving Chinese citizens a "better life."

Challenge for China

With a population already exceeding 1.4 billion, a change to democracy would be a challenge for China. Could a parliament effectively represent this number of people? Would political change continue to support the country's recent economic progress? These are just some of the questions standing in the way of democratic reform in the Asian superpower.

Democracy in Action

While it is unlikely that China will become a democracy, some people believe that the country's rapid economic growth may affect its political future. The growth has greatly increased the wealth of the millions of people who have moved from rural areas to the cities, to work in factories. They have money to spend on goods and services. Car sales, for example, have escalated. In 2020, one in every three cars sold worldwide was sold to a customer in China.

Do you think that people with more financial independence are likely to want more political opportunities, too?

Will wealthier people feel they deserve to have more of a say in how their country is run?

PAST AND PRESENT:

Can you imagine a time when the people of China demand a move away from their past political system and demand democracy? How do you think that might come about?

CONCLUSION

Democracy Past, Present, and Future

We have learned that democracy as a system of government has a very long history, but that the struggle to achieve it has been difficult. In some countries, democracy evolved over centuries. Other countries have tried to impose democracy quickly, in reaction to an oppressive government. Many countries are still without democracy, and the world's most widespread political system still faces many challenges in the modern world.

An Expectation of Rights and Freedom

People living in a democracy can expect to enjoy freedom of expression and the protection of their human rights, including equality of opportunity regardless of gender, religion, or race. However, the people need to play an important role, too. Democracies can only work effectively when both politicians and voters are actively involved in the decision-making process.

These students protested on the streets of London, UK, about the rising cost of university fees. They hoped their actions would persuade the government to change its policies.

These Argentinians are showing their support for a new president who has vowed to represent their interests.

All national democracies are representative: the people elect politicians to represent them for a period of a few years. The executive branch makes policy decisions, the legislature debates those policies and makes laws, and the judiciary then safeguards the use of the law equally, to all people in the country.

Delicate Democracy

Democracy is more fragile in some countries than others. In the West, for example, some people show signs of taking their democracy for granted, and losing interest in politics. In other countries, the people are fighting to gain the right to have a say in their government. However, most people agree that democracy is here to stay. Many people and organizations around the world are working to improve people's access to democracy, and to overcome the future challenges this hard-won system faces.

Democracy in Action

British prime minister Sir Winston Churchill said in 1947, "Democracy is the worst form of government except all the others that have been tried from time to time." What he meant was that no form of government can be perfect.

Democracy may be the most tried and tested political system, but does it stand up to the test?

How well do you think the world's democracies perform, in protecting the rights of citizens, and in giving them effective, stable government?

How do you think Churchill's words can be applied to the democratic countries we have looked at around the world in this book?

Glossary

abolition to get rid of something, to make it illegal
absolute rule to rule without any challenge to one's authority
authoritarian a form of rule in which the opinion of others is not considered
barons men who held a lot of land during the medieval period
cabinet the meeting of members of the executive branch, or ministers
censoring controlling the information that people in a country receive
Civil Rights Movement a movement that fought for equality for Black people in the United States in the 1960s
coalition the joining of two or more political parties in order to rule
colonies countries that are ruled over by another country, as part of an empire
communism a system of government where the state controls all wealth and property
constitution a set of rules and principles that lays down how a nation should be governed
dictatorship government by a leader who rules with absolute power
direct democracy a system in which all the people make everyday decisions of government
discrimination excluding someone because of their gender, race, age, or religious beliefs
elite a group of people with privileges not available to everyone
executive branch the branch of government that creates policy and carries it out
fascism a political movement in favor of dictatorial, repressive government
federation a group of organizations or countries that join to enforce power or order
franchise the right to vote
hierarchical organized by rank, with the most powerful at the top
human rights rights that every human being has, regardless of gender, race, or religion
judiciary the branch of government consisting of the judges and law courts
jury a group of ordinary citizens called upon in a court of law to decide whether the tried person is guilty or innocent
legislature the branch of government that debates policy and makes laws
minister a person who is elected to help govern a country
monarchy rule by a king or queen, who usually inherits their role
nobility the upper classes in a monarchy
oppressive controlling with force
radicals people with extreme beliefs
referendum a vote open to all citizens on an issue of national importance

reform political or social change

representative democracy a system in which the people elect politicians to represent them in government

republic a democracy in which the head of state is also elected, rather than a hereditary monarch

revolution a violent upheaval to overthrow a ruler or bring radical change

socialism a political system in which wealth is shared equally between the people

sovereignty supreme authority over a country

Soviet Union a union of countries in Eastern Europe, led by Russia, which lasted until 1991

suffrage the right to vote. Universal suffrage is the right of all adults to vote

Find Out More

Books

Foster, Jeff. *For Which We Stand: How Our Government Works and Why it Matters*. Scholastic, 2020.

Rusch, Elizabeth. *You Call This Democracy?: How to Fix Our Government and Deliver Power to the People*. Clarion Books, 2020.

Sheehan, Ben. *What Does the Constitution Say? A Kid's Guide to How Our Democracy Works*. Black Dog & Leventhal, 2021.

Websites

Discover more about modern democracy at:
www.democracyculturefoundation.org

Find out more about the origins of democracy and its place in our world today at:
education.nationalgeographic.org/resource/democracy-ancient-greece

Some useful videos about democracy can be found at:
www.neok12.com/Democracy.htm

Publisher's note to educators and parents:
All the websites featured above have been carefully reviewed to ensure that they are suitable for students. However, many websites change often, and we cannot guarantee that a site's future contents will continue to meet our high standards of educational value. Please be advised that students should be closely monitored whenever they access the Internet.

Index

ABOUT THE AUTHOR

Alex Webb has written many children's books and has a particular interest in history and politics. She has found researching and writing this book fascinating and hopes that it helps students everywhere gain knowledge and insight into political systems and how they work.